CRA-ACK, THE CROW

By
Lyle Cowles

TEACH Services, Inc.
P U B L I S H I N G
www.TEACHServices.com • (800) 367-1844

Copyright © 2008, 2018 TEACH Services, Inc.
ISBN-13: 978-1-57258-484-6 (Paperback)
Library of Congress Control Number: 2007942148

TEACH Services, Inc.
P U B L I S H I N G
www.TEACHServices.com • (800) 367-1844

CONTENTS

To Mom And Dad,
Grandma And Grandpa Kaemmle,
And All The Cowles kids
Past, Present and Future.

Jessica Evelyn Cowles Gow-Lee, Editor

Much thanks to my husband, Guillermo Gow-Lee for the hours of work scanning the pictures and helping me set this story up on the computer. I wish, Dad, that you could have seen this, your second book. You would have liked it! I look forward to the day when we can see you again and you can meet all the new members of your family.

I. OUR HOME BY THE RIVER

My mother was beautiful.

I can remember sitting in our soft lined bird nest high in the crotch of an alder tree along the banks of the Sol Duc River with my sister and brother. We could look over the edge of the nest down through the branches at the ground far below. Then we could see ever farther because the branches would lift and the leaves would turn and we could see stretches of the sparkling river.

There was a trail down there. It was usually deserted on rainy days, but when the sun shone warm and bright we would see people walking along the trail. They did not know we were there. That was just as well, Ma said, for people were not to be trusted.

She—that is, Ma, used to make regular trips to our nest. She would sit on the big broken limb along by one edge and she always had a fat grub or a grasshopper or some other juicy tid-bit dear to the stomachs of us wee young-ones. Ma was black and shiny and full of life. She would not put up with nonsense, though, and when people were about down below she made us be quiet.

We lived several weeks in our treetop. The nest seemed to get smaller every day, or may-

1

be we were growing larger. Anyway, things kept getting more crowded all the time. Soon there just wasn't room enough no matter which way we turned. When Ma came with a good beak-full of goodies it was all we could do to keep from falling out, what with our pushing and reaching to make sure we got our share—and someone else's share, too, if we could get away with it. Ma was very provoked with our greediness at times. She'd just poke the food down the first mouth she came to and fly off to get more.

Sometimes she would be gone for a long time. We would see other Mas flitting through the trees and hear the greedy gobbling of other young crows in trees here and there through the grove. I don't know what took Ma so long. Perhaps she just wanted to rest and gossip with the rest of the flock.

With Ma gone so long Brother and Sister and I got to creeping out of the nest a bit farther every day. One day we got all the way out. Ma certainly was surprised to come back and find us all out and sitting in a row on the broken limb.

She was happy that we were getting so strong, but she cautioned us to hold on tight, for if we should fall to the ground she would not be able to get us back into the tree and would have to feed us down there. And there were so many more dangers for young and helpless birds that had the misfortune to fall to the ground.

Ma told us about cats and dogs and coons and skunks—and people. The people often had dogs with them, big ones and little ones, black ones, brown ones and white ones. The dogs and the little people were always tearing off through the brushes helter-skelter, the dogs snuffling and digging and the little people making such an awful racket. It certainly was exciting! But the big people just poked along and didn't make much noise at all except to call to the little people to make them behave.

Those little people—they weren't like my brother and sister and me. When Ma told us something, we did it! She seemed to know what was best and we listened. Those young people, though, sometimes it seemed as if they didn't even hear their parents. Sometimes I think the dogs were better trained. At least they left off their snuffling and digging when they were called.

We never did see any cats or coons or skunks. Ma said they always come around at night. All good birds are high in trees after dark and are reasonably safe from the night prowling land animals. At night we could often hear faint splashes along the margin of the river. Ma said those noises were made by coons hunting for periwinkles and crawfish among the riverside stones. Then one night when the moon was bright we heard faint chirring sounds and we could see, down against the black of the ground, some faint white spots moving along. Ma said it was a family of skunks moving along single-file through the trees.

There was never any sign of cats, but from what Ma told us, I was sure I would know one if I saw it. When I grew older I did get acquainted with cats, but now I am getting ahead of my story. I will tell you about cats later.

One morning, right after sun-up, we squeezed out of the nest and on up our perching limb as was getting to be our habit. It was a fine day. Smoke from the camps of the people drifted down through the trees. Sometimes a little breeze stirred the tops and our tree rocked gently. Ma was feeding us regularly and everything was just wonderful. As the day grew warmer the people and dogs began to come by below on the trail. They didn't bother us, though, for when they were in sight we just kept quiet and they didn't even look up.

Suddenly there was a *swish* and a *thunk* up overhead. It frightened us for a moment until we saw it was only a squirrel. A squirrel is a little animal—with four feet—and no wings at all. He can't get around in the trees nearly as well as we birds can and Ma could certainly chase him away any time she chose, which would be whenever she saw him. She says birds can't trust squirrels either, for they will steal eggs if they have the chance.

Well, this squirrel saw us, too, sitting on our limb. We were far from being in the egg stage and wouldn't be legitimate prey for a squirrel. He knew this, of course, but, being as Ma wasn't around he just had to tease us.

He came head first down our perch limb, chattering, twitching his tail, and making all kinds of threats. We weren't at all afraid of him and told him he had better be on his way for Ma would be back any moment and would make things quite uncomfortable for him.

The squirrel didn't pay us any mind. He just came closer—so close we couldn't abide him any more. Brother crowded down against Sister, Sister crowded down against me. I didn't like that at all for there wasn't anything for me to hold to and if they kept pushing I was bound to fall off the broken end of the limb.

I pushed back, and with all the pushing and scrambling, and beating of wings, and that horrible squirrel crowding us more and more, there just wasn't any help for us. We fell from the limb.

II. I BEGIN A NEW LIFE

The fall from the tree wasn't too bad, but rather scary. I bounced off a few limbs at first but near the bottom of the tree it was quite open. Instinct told me to spread my wings, and, though I only had some down and some pinfeathers, my action prevented me from plowing into the ground at full speed.

I landed in a bunch of sword ferns. I was so frightened at the strangeness of my surroundings that I could do nothing but stay as still as possible. Brother and Sister were nowhere in sight, and I suppose they were as afraid as I was and staying just as still.

Ma came back then. I couldn't see her, but I did hear her cry out for us. And there was an awful commotion when she saw the squirrel and realized what had happened. I think that terrible animal escaped with his life, but just barely.

Ma came down to the lower branches and began to call us. I didn't say anything. I wiggled out of the sword ferns and just sat there, hoping she would see me. She did—and she found Brother and Sister, too. She was quite unhappy at our predicament, for, as she had told us before, our chances of survival on the ground were very small.

For several hours Ma came back with food for us. She had to be very careful. The trail was close by and people were constantly passing. If only the dogs would stay away.

It had been quiet for some time. Ma had just left after feeding us. Suddenly we heard a shout—and knew at once that it was one of the little people.

"There's a baby raven!" the voice said.

Bearing down on us was one of the little people, but he didn't look so little from down there on the ground. I tried frantically to get away. But the boy, for that is what it was, was too fast for me. He raced through the ferns and bushes as if they were not there at all! If I had had my wing feathers I am sure I could have eluded him.

As it was, one of his big hands pinned me to the ground. I was not hurt, but nearly suffocated from fright. I pecked at his fingers. He just laughed and slid his other hand beneath me. I was air-borne again, but I couldn't move my wings or feet at all, only my head where it stuck out from between his fingers.

There was nothing I could do. The boy carried me, trying to keep me away from several other little people who kept crowding around, saying "Oh" and "Ah" and "Let me see him!" and poking their fingers at my face until I tried to get out of sight by squirming back into the warm pocket of his hands.

Then there was smoke from campfires and dogs running around and people—people everywhere, big ones and little ones.

I heard one big one say, "What do you have there, Ivan?"

The boy holding me said, "I think it's a baby raven, Dad! Where's that dollar you were going to give me if I caught one for you?"

Dad came over then and he poked his finger at me, too, and after a little bit he said, "That's not a raven, Ivan, that is only a crow!"

Well, I am glad they finally realized I was not a raven, but I didn't really care for that "only a crow" remark. I wiggled some more, trying to get away, but it just was no use.

The people discussed me for awhile and referred to a big lady they called "Mama." Then they decided not to take me back to the woods again, which was probably just as well, for I don't think they could have found where they caught me, and I am sure Ma had given me up anyway when she found what had happened.

The people stuck me in a box. It was dark and hot and stuffy in there and just a little slit of light came in where the cover didn't come quite shut. I tried at first to get out through that slit, but when I did I could see people looking down at the hole. I knew they would grab at me again if I got out, so I just crowded back in a corner and hoped they would forget about me.

After awhile there was a rumbling noise. I know we were moving. Then the rumbling stopped and I felt the box being lifted and carried somewhere. The cover was opened. I just looked up at those people and said "Ah-ah-ah!" and they closed the cover again. I could hear lots of noises and talking.

That evening they took me out of the box—Ivan did that is, and put me in another box—only this one was made of wire and was full of holes so I could see out. There were soft rags in one corner and people looking at me again. I couldn't hide; there was no place to get out of sight.

Then one of the people said something about feeding me. That was all right with me, but I didn't know what they would give me to eat. Whatever it was, I was sure I wouldn't like it.

Ivan reached in and picked me up. I turned my head away when he tried to poke something at my face. Then Dad took hold of my head and squeezed his fingers. I couldn't help it. My beak just popped open, and they dribbled some stuff down my throat. It really wasn't bad at all—and later on, when I decided that eating was more pleasant than going hungry, I found that this stuff was boiled egg yolk.

Later on they fed me all kinds of stuff; bread and dog food and all and I felt myself growing stronger all the while.

One time, one of the girls—I soon learned there were three in the house, Susie, Joan, and Jessica—well, Joan it was, was squirting water down my throat with a medicine dropper. I liked the water, but I thought that was a strange way to get it. Well, this medicine dropper slipped from her fingers and I just swallowed it, the whole thing.

I was quite amused, for Joan thought something terrible was going to happen. She ran and told the big Mama, and everybody came and looked at me, making clucking noises and shaking their heads.

Soon they left me alone. From what they said I knew they thought I was done for, but I just smiled to myself and when no one was looking I just *urped* and up came the medicine dropper. They were certainly surprised when they found it in the bottom of the cage!

III. I LEARN TO FLY

I learned to like this family I had been kid-napped to live with. They always handled me gently, and, what was quite important, they fed me quite regularly. Of course it wasn't the same food that Ma would have brought to me, but considering that these were only people, and not having the sense of a good Ma crow, they did the best they could.

Egg yolks, bread, and canned dog food seemed only poor substitutes for bugs and grubs and occasional pieces of good red meat from some rabbit or squirrel that had met its end on the highway, but in spite of that I began to thrive.

My wing feathers grew long and shiny. Those on my head and breast began to smooth out and I often heard my new family exclaim how the light reflected in so many rainbow colors from my new feathers. There were still bits of fuzz feathers sticking out in the oddest places, but all in all I felt I was beginning to look like a crow ought to look.

Sometimes one of the children would ne-glect to close the top of my cage. At such times I would hop to the edge and from there over on to Ivan or David's bed. David was Ivan's brother. He was not as big as Ivan was, but

13

he was interested in me, too. That's what I really liked—people who were interested in me.

Occasionally I would miss the bed and land, kerplunk, on the floor. I didn't like floors. They were always slippery with wax so I couldn't get a good foothold. I would go skittering and skating along the smooth surface without being able to get set good enough to try my wings.

There were interesting things on the floor though— buttons, pieces of paper, Jessica's crayons, and sometimes a nice long piece of string to pull around behind me.

A real treasure trove was the boys' dressers. On them were all kinds of shiny things.

My special favorites were the pieces of bright colored plastic which Ivan was always tinkering with; gluing them together to make boats and cars and what-not. In all the time I have lived in this house I have never understood why he got so excited about the few little pieces I took. He had many more—more, I am sure, than he really needed.

Sometimes Dad, or David, or Ivan would take me into the big main room of the house and set me on the back of a chair. I would sit there for a few minutes, then try for the table. I didn't do so well at first, but before long I was able to fly around the room quite well.

On sunshiny days I was taken outside where one of the boys would toss me into the air and I would sail for a good distance.

The most thrilling experience of my flight training came one bright day. It didn't seem so nice at first. Ivan stuck me inside his shirt. It was almost suffocating in there. I scrambled around and peeked and squawked and tried to get out between the buttons. I was sure that boy was up to no good.

He carried me in his shirt for fifteen minutes or so, then took me out. Lo and behold, I was high in a tree again! At least as high as my old nest had been. The ground looked a frightening distance down. I am a bird, though, and shouldn't really admit to being afraid in high places.

Ivan held me a moment in his hand, then tossed me out into the air! I tumbled some, then got my bearings in time to make quite a respectable flight. Out into space! Grandpa Kaemmle's barn roof passed below me and I was losing altitude fast. Ahead of me was a grove of fruit trees. I knew I would probably take a tumble if I tried to land on a limb. My control was still too poor for close maneuvering, so I turned to the garden patch instead. I managed to clear the pea vines by just inches and made my landing in the strawberry patch.

It wasn't long before I could do without being tossed into the air. I could take off from most anywhere all by myself. Landing was more difficult. Wires were so thin and wriggly and tree branches always seemed to have other twigs and limbs to foul up my approach. I found the best landing areas were the tops of houses or barns, or fence posts.

IV. PLAYMATES

Now that I was reasonably self-sufficient in getting about the home place, I was given much more freedom. For ever longer periods of time the Family allowed me out of the cage. I began to take note of the other inhabitants of this farm.

There were two kittens. One was "Mrs. Grey," a black and white longhaired kitten of dubious ancestry. The other was a mostly Siamese cat, which the girls had named "Samantha," but that Dad always called "Supe." He said that was short for "Supercalifragilistic-expialidocious," which should have been her name in the first place.

I had great sport with the kittens. They couldn't fly, of course, and were easy marks for just about any teasing I cared to give them. Sometimes they would go mincing across the yard with their tails sticking straight up in the air, perfect little handles for me to grab!

I would sail softly across the yard, just above the grass until I got within good reach, then give that supercilious tail a good tweak with my beak! Oh, how the kittens did yowl and turn on their backs to swat at me! I would just sail to a fence post, shake the kitten fur from my beak and chuckle to myself.

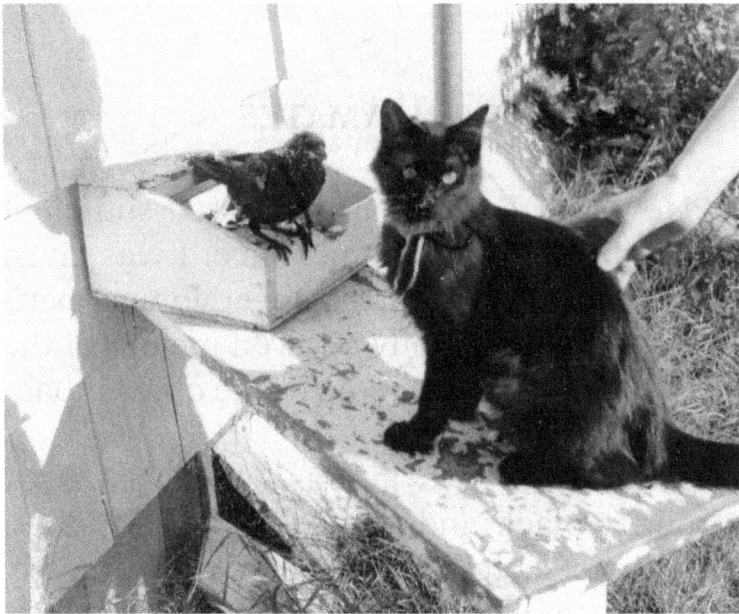

Kittens have a way of becoming cats. As they grew larger I realized there might be real danger in those clawed front paws. I remembered what Ma said about cats and decided to be more cautious around them. It finally came to the place where I dared not pull their tails unless I found them asleep.

Beside the path on the way to the barn is a small hutch where "Bugs" lives. "Bugs" is a rabbit. Most of the time she has the run of the yard and hops here and there munching tufts of grass and wiggling her nose. Mama sometimes becomes upset when Bugs gets into the carrot patch. Then poor Bugs finds herself confined to the hutch again—until Mama cools down.

I sit on the eaves of the hutch and by hanging down just a bit I can see Bugs in there. She doesn't seem to mind being cooped up as long as she has grass or vegetables to munch on.

Times she is out she works on her burrow. That is over by Jessica's swing. I saw Ivan try to measure the burrow once. He poked a pole in several feet before he reached a turning point and couldn't get it in any further.

I started to follow Bugs into her burrow one day. I could see her away back in there, but she soon disappeared around a bend and I decided that burrows just aren't meant for crows so I gave up.

On cold days it is fun to get on the horses' backs. There are two horses. One is a pinto,

whom Dad is forever calling "Hobbin, the rorse." This is just a play on words for the pinto is really "Robin" the horse. I'd gathered that Robin does not much care to be called "Hobbin," but he stands for it because of his fond regard for Dad. They had worked together for many years in Olympic National Park. Robin assured me that he had carried Dad for thousands of miles on trails through the mountains.

The other horse is a relative newcomer, though he had lived there for a long while before I arrived. He belongs to Joan. His name is "Gold-Dust", but Joan affectionately refers to him as "Disgust."

Gold-Dust is not very old, as horses' years go, but he is rather intelligent. Not as wise as we crows, of course, but smart considering that he is only a horse.

I become rather irritated at him sometimes. Joan will play with him—show off his tricks, such as bowing, hand-shaking and thing like that—and feed him apples—and pay no attention to me at all.

When the horses are in the pasture grazing around on the grass, (why they like to eat that stuff, I will never know!), I sometimes sit on one's back. If I stay quiet it is likely that I can have some fun chasing blackbirds. They have a custom of following around close under a horse's nose, catching insects that are chased up when the horses pull out the grass.

I bide my time, and just at the right moment pounce down upon the blackbirds. Startled, they fly up and I give them a merry chase! Around the pasture, up through the big maple tree, then across the pasture over Grandpa's garage, up the road and over the Family's house—then I have to give up. Blackbirds are small and hard to catch!

Speaking of birds, some I just can not abide. Like those swallows that live in the

garage, and the others that nest in boxes that Dad has put up for them. Swallows will not leave me alone. If I sit comfortably on a fence post, or amuse myself at all, they surely see me and attack. They dive so close to me, and make such shrill chirpings that it is impossible to ignore them.

The best thing about swallows is that they don't stay the year around. Where they disappear to in the fall I have no idea, but I am glad when they go.

April is a cow, a brown, stubby-horned, cud-chewing animal that doesn't have very good sense. Seems like her only interest is in eating grass, especially the grass on the other side of the fence.

Fences don't mean anything to me for I just fly over them. With these poor ground-bound four legged animals—and most of the time even to people, fences are barriers they have to cross by means of gates.

Close by Dad's workshop is a gate. A swinging gate latched with a sliding wooden two-by-four and locked by means of a large nail that is pushed through a hole in the gate frame and through a corresponding hole in the sliding two-by-four.

This large nail has always fascinated me because it is secured to the gatepost by a leather thong. Try as I might, I have never been able to steal that nail. I can pull it out of the hole, but I can not take it away.

Several times I have caused some excitement, (I do like things exciting!) by pulling out this lock nail while April was by the gate. April seemed to be aware that the sliding bar keeps the gate shut. If none of the Family is looking she will hook one of her stubby little horns behind the handle of the sliding bar— and slide it. The gate swings open and April has free access to the lawn and garden—until one of the Family catches sight of her!

What a "to-do" of cow chasing there is then! And it certainly is fun!

The Family dog is Midnight. Just as black as I am, he is. Midnight doesn't like me much but I really do not care as long as he doesn't try to catch me. That he could is not very likely. He can move faster than April, the cow can, but he can't reach very high.

Perhaps he doesn't care for me because I find his food so tempting. I know that he keeps a very close watch on me when I am by his food dish. Midnight is old and likes to sleep. When he sleeps I gorge on dog food.

I can't eat it all, but I can hide it. Many quiet mornings when the Family is slow to get out of bed I can have breakfast by going to some of my dog food caches.

I am not the only one who steals Midnight's food, though. A huge black Labrador named Sambo is a frequent raider of the dog dish. Sambo does not belong on the Place. He lives down by the river at some neighbor people's house. I scold Sambo a lot for his thievery, but he doesn't pay any heed to me. Midnight does not like Sambo either, but he is too small to do anything about it.

One day he tried to fight with Sambo. All he got out of the fight was a broken jaw that did not mend right, so now Midnight has one side of his mouth that doesn't match the other. Mama calls him "Gee-whopper-jaw."

V. RIGHT AROUND HOME

People are more dear to me than any other creatures, especially the people of my Family. People call me a crow, but I have lived in a house with the Family. They have fed me and played with me and protected me when I was young. I know I look and act like a crow, but I know also that I am one of the Family.

I have often seen great flocks of crows flying about the Place. I have heard them calling and talking to each other. Other crows do

29

not interest me. I did try to get acquainted when I first got my wings and even went so far as to fly back to the grove at the Tumbling Rapids camp on the river. I found the old nest. Ma wasn't around, nor my brother and sister, so I went home to the Family again.

I had been gone for several days, just visiting different homes of people along the highway around Tyee and Sappho.

Mornings I would be hungry. Not having any caches in that part of the country I decided to beg some food from strangers. I found that by perching on the windowsills of the houses. I could arouse their interest and usually they would bring me some food.

I had to be cautious, though. Many people tried to catch me. I did not like that. I am sure they would not hurt me, but one thing I have never cared for is to be imprisoned in a person's hands—even in the hands of the Family.

I decided it was time to return to the home Place after the following item appeared in the local weekly paper, the Forks Forum:

> Lost crow, a family pet. Thought to be in the Beaver area. Likes to beg at windows for food. If seen, please don't try to catch him. Call the Cowles family at 374-5151 and we will come and take him home.

You see, the Family missed me. I am not ungrateful, but we crows like to travel.

After my adventure away from home I was glad to be back again, back to my old perch on the back porch, or the one in Dad's workshop.

Sometimes it is difficult to decide which is the better place to spend the night. I might get all settled down on the back porch, then Dad will go out in the dark to his workshop. I hear him hammering or grinding—tinkering, he calls it—and I decide the workshop is a more interesting place to sit.

There are many intriguing things in the workshop, nails and screws and bolts and all sorts of other things. Dad likes to have me around out there. He talks to me and rubs my neck and lets me know I am welcome, but sometimes he seems very selfish about his tools and motor parts. Always putting them in drawers or cans with lids on.

One afternoon I had a bad time in that workshop. Dad was grinding an axe on the emery wheel. I was young and foolish then and didn't know about such things as emery wheels. Such a beautiful shower of white sparks flew from the grinder that I decided I must have some. What I did no know was that the wheel was turning so rapidly. Well, I went after the sparks all right! Before Dad could bat me away I landed on the turning grindstone! Bz-z-z-z it went on my leg! Oh, how painful! Needless to say I left the workshop as soon as I could fly. The long scrape on my leg healed in time, but I will never trust an emery wheel again!

Most mornings the Family is up bright and early. Other mornings such as those on weekends, I think they will <u>never</u> get out of bed!

Sometimes things are so lonesome in the early daylight that I have to do something to arouse them. Pecking on the window often works, especially on Ivan's window. He is not as particular as Mama or Dad about birds in the house.

Ivan will slide his window open and I hop in on to his bed and talk to him. I like to have my head rubbed with a finger. That does something to me. Ivan likes it, too, for when I make that noise Dad says is like half a pigeon "coo," Ivan laughs and rubs me some more—perhaps under my beak, which is a good place to get rubbed, too.

On sunny days the Family spends most of the time outside where I have a chance to play with them. We have several games. One is a teasing game, I guess. One of the children, or maybe Mama or Dad will wave a straw or a leaf and I will try to catch it in my beak as I fly by.

Sometimes one of the family will attract my attention with a small object, usually something bright, which I can not resist. After arousing my interest they will hide the

object—as if I can't see what they are doing!
Well—I will locate the little trinket and find
my own hiding place somewhere in the grass.
I peck a little hole down in the grass and en-
large it by inserting my beak and opening it,
then carefully stow the object out of sight. To
make certain it is well hidden I cover it over
with leaves or small sticks and start off very
satisfied with myself,

Whoever is playing the game with me then
hunts for the object and removes it from my
little cache. Of course I act very indignant
and insist on having it back, whereupon they
hide it again—and I find it. This goes on until
one of us tires of it and finds something else
to do.

Ivan built a swing down by the river. He
attached a large rope to a big limb high up
in an alder tree. Whole gangs of children enjoy that swing. Grasping the rope with both
hands, they leap in the air from the high
bank, wrap their legs around the rope above
the stick tied in the end for a seat and swing
in a great arc out over the water of the river.
It seems fun to them. They scream with delight.

I really do not see much to be excited about
with such a short spin in the air. I can swoop
much farther with far less effort.

The rope, where it is tied to the big limb,
did interest me, though. It creaks back and

forth, partially unwinding where it coiled around the limb each time the child swings outwards. I was curious as to what is under this rope with all the squeaking and popping.

One day I sat on the limb by the rope. Each time the rope swung outward I peered under it, stretching farther and farther, but I still could not see what made the squeaking noise. As the rope returned in its arc, the gap between the rope and the limb would close again.

To make my story short—I did something very foolish. I neglected to pull my head out from beneath the rope quite soon enough. The gap closed as the rope swung back and caught my beak! Oh what a painful predicament! I flapped and clawed and squawked but could not get out for what seemed such a long time while the rope swung out again to release me.

I flew, somewhat erratically I am afraid, back to the house. Later Dad looked my beak over and decided that though it was flattened a little on the end, it would probably be all right with time to heal. Needless to say—I'll not play around that rope again.

Don't think I spend all my time at play. I have other things to do, too. I like to take a bath in the puddles by the lawn sprinkler and then to sit on a fence post in the sunshine and shake and preen each feather dry. With a little time spent caring for myself I keep shiny black, glossy and neat looking.

When Dad is away working, and the children are I don't know where, I spend a great deal of time helping Mama with her work— that is, her outside work. She frowns on my spending much time inside the house. Why, I don't exactly know—except that when I am in there, there is always someone following me around with a rag-wiping the floor.

I do delight at helping Mama pick peas. I sit on her head and show her where all the good ones are, then when she pulls them from the vine and puts them in the bucket, I hop down and peck them open.

When she shells the peas I get into the pot of shelled ones and help myself. I can hold just so many of them though. When I reach my capacity I fly over to the edge of the garden where she can't see me and regurgitate the peas. I am empty then, and can go back for another helping.

I help Mama with the wash sometimes. She doesn't always appreciate what I do, but my intentions are good.

She brought the basket of wet clothes to the back yard one morning. There were an awful lot of them in the basket. I could see it would take her a long time to hang all those things on the line. I looked over the clothes, picked and pulled at some, and found that shirts and sheets are heavier than I can manage, but socks are just my size.

I picked out a nice, white sock and started for the clothesline with it. Mama must have misunderstood my intentions for she made a grab for the sock. I was too quick for her. I ducked away and flew to the top of the garage.

Mama yelled at me a few times. I don't think she was too pleased. After a while she calmed down and proceeded to hang out the rest of the clothes. To show my good intentions I took the sock and flew over to the clothesline—up high where she could not reach me. I landed on a sheet and was about to hang the sock on the line when she moved the line. In trying to keep my balance I lost the sock. Quick as a wink Mama was there and grabbed it. If that is going to be her attitude I just won't help her with the wash any more!

Clothes on the line can be great fun! Especially those that have long strings hanging from them. I fly up and grab the string and swing to and fro—just like the children on the rope swing down by the river.

Dangling strings have a particular attraction for me. I had the Family mystified for a while by turning on the back porch light. It is a pull-chain switch and has a button on the end. This button is just the right size to catch with my beak.

Many were the times I have heard Dad say: "Who turned the porch light on?" I think that is a good trick.

When I stay around the Place things go quite well with me, but when I visit the neighbors I seem to get in trouble. Not always, but sometimes. Our neighbors across the road, the Claytons, are always good to me. I land on their kitchen window sill, bang on the window a few times with my beak and Cam, that is, Mrs. Clayton, is almost sure to bring me out some food, some scraps of meat or bread. It is usually worth while to visit the Claytons.

I did my reputation a bad turn one day over there, though. Cam was sitting on her front steps shelling peas, and I was helping the best I could. Well, Cam decided to rest a minute. She took out her cigarettes, put one in her mouth, and reached for her lighter. That is a strange habit that so many people have! I know it is not a good thing to do. I can't imagine a self-respecting crow smoking a cigarette!

I jumped up, grabbed the cigarette from Cam's mouth and flew out in the yard with it. Cam was so surprised! The cigarette didn't taste good at all, so I tore it all to little pieces. Cam watched me with interest while she took out another one and lit it.

Later on I happened to be sitting on the front porch railing at home while Cam was inside visiting Mama. She told Mama that I ate her cigarette and wasn't a good Christian crow! There went my reputation!

Visiting some other neighbors down the road got me into more serious trouble. These neighbors have a small daughter. She has such long beautiful blonde hair and it is such a delight to pull! Whenever I could find her out-of-doors I would fly quietly to a good vantage point, then dive to her head. How she would squeal and run! Of course the girl's mother complained to Mama and the first thing I knew I had one of my wings clipped! That was a miserable situation! No more sailing from porch to barn roof or from tree to tree, just awkward flutterings from the ground to fence post. I tell you—I had to keep a close watch for Sambo and the cats then!

So the summer passed and the time of my greatest adventures drew near.

VI. I GO TO SCHOOL

Every morning, five days a week during the winter, a big yellow bus stops at the corner by the Place. The children get on this bus and are gone all day long.

The weather was getting bad. With no children around, and Dad gone to work, and with Mama staying in the house out of the rain and wind most of the time, it got to be rather lonesome.

Every morning I waited with the children and watched them get on the bus. I did not know where they went. After so much of this I decided to follow the bus to see if I could be near the children. So I did.

The bus was easy to follow. The great, noisy yellow monster snorted up the highway. Though it traveled most of the time at a greater speed than I could comfortably fly, it made so many stops to load children that I was well able to keep it in sight.

The bus went east to Tyee, where it turned around and went back towards home. I thought it would stop there, but it didn't. Instead it continued west. Soon it came to a small town. There were more houses there than I had ever seen in my whole life. Buildings, and lights and wires and people.

The bus's final stop was by a group of huge brick buildings with children everywhere. They were running and shouting—excitement enough to delight the heart of any crow! Here were children on swings and slides, throwing balls and dropping pencils. This looked like fun. And fun it was. I like children and the things they do.

Shortly after the bus arrived a bell rang and all the children went inside. It was certainly quiet then. No activity.

Through the windows I could see them, sitting in great long rows, waving papers—and laughing and pointing at me as I sat on the window sill

I soon located an open window and went inside, much to the enjoyment of the children, and later on, to the consternation of the big people, one of whom seemed to be in each room.

These big people chased me out of room after room. When one room was closed to me I would search about the building until I found another open window and in I would go again.

The best room of all had bottles and jars, full of beautifully colored stuff. What a delightful crash they made when I knocked them from the tables!

It was not long before I felt that I was unwelcome inside with the children, so I waited outside until they came out to play again. Then we had fun.

One day a notice came out in the bulletin of the school, for that is what it was. It went like this.

> Please don't try to hurt or catch the crow that comes looking in your classrom windows and plays with you on the playground. He is a pet of Ivan and David Cowles and doesn't like to be caught or held.

Protected to a degree by the bulletin my life was a lot easier and I decided to stay around the school indefinitely. Every evening the buses would come and the children would leave, leaving me nothing to do but to try to find food. Of course, the children fed me during the day, but we crows do like to eat—and, as I said before, when we get filled we can always urp ourselves empty again, all the better to enjoy some more.

In addition to the Family children there was one boy at the school that I especially was fond of. His name was John Leibold. This boy seemed to have an affinity for crows and I learned to trust him more than the other children. I suppose we crows have extra sensory perception that tells us when we may be flirting with danger and who we can put our confidence in. Anyway, I liked Leibold.

I soon learned that he lived in a large white house in the town and made it a point to visit him after school. This was better than flying all the way home for meals in the evening.

My new friend had to go to bed in the evenings at an earlier hour than I cared to. The lights on the main street of the town attracted me so I decided to investigate. Soon I knew my way around the town quite well and found a number of things to do there.

One of the brightest windows in town was the one in front of a cafe called the Vagabond. Here there was a convenient window ledge, near the door and under a cocktail sign.

The patrons of the cafe were pleased to see me. I would strut up and down the ledge and peer in the window and make chuckling noises. As the people came out they would lay all sorts of tasty tid-bits on the ledge for me. I did not lack for food.

With plenty of food and all the enjoyment I had with the children at school each day I had no thought of returning home. I was with the Family children at school each day, too, and that was enough for me.

VII. I CHANGE COLORS

Even good things come to an end.

Naturally some of the children tried to catch me. My experience to date with the younger set enabled me to perceive their interest and I was always able to elude them. This exasperated some of the ruder children and they would work out their frustrations by throwing sticks, or whatever came to hand, at me.

Along about this time my fame was enhanced by being the subject of a printed article for the third time in my life. This time it was a school bulletin put out by the principal. It read as follows:

> To the students: If you see a tame crow, don't throw anything at it, or try to catch it. He is a pet of David Cowles and his family. The bird has two aluminum bands around his leg.

One day after school as I was playing with some boys I became careless and was caught. I pecked and squawked and struggled with all my might, but it was hopeless. I could not escape.

I was carried to their home and kept, an unwilling prisoner, in a box for several days.

I am sure the school children and the Family missed me, but there was nothing I could do.

Though these people fed me, I did not trust them, for I knew there was mischief in their hearts. Mischief there was—and of just about the worst kind for one of my beauty and dignity. It was paint they were thinking of—red for my wings and blue for my legs. Perhaps their idea was that this would make me easier to spot as a tame crow. Crows are supposed to be black, tame or wild, not red and blue. That is for parrots!

I did not stay in their captivity long after the paint job. I made my way back to school where I became the object of commiseration to my friends.

The family soon heard of my disgrace and the first thing I knew I was back at the Place with a wing clipped. I was assured this was just until I had time to grow a new set of feathers.

VIII. I GO TO SCHOOL AGAIN

There was time to grow new feathers all right. Winter came and passed—snow and cold rain.

I sat, huddled up most of the time, in a large cage Dad had set for me near the back porch. I hated that cage, but with a clipped wing, and cats and dogs around, I guess it was the best place for me.

Dad put a larger piece of plywood on top of the cage to keep the rain off me, and other pieces beside the cage to shelter me from the wind. Though I detested being cooped up, I was quite comfortable. I was fed twice a day and there was always a dish of water to quench my thirst.

49

Caged life is awfully boring. The most excitement I had was scolding the neighbor's big yellow tom cat that would so like to catch me, but couldn't through the wires of my prison. He had to content himself with salvaging scraps of food I had been careless enough to allow to drop through to the ground below.

As the weather became more mild during the latter part of March the Family would occasionally open the cage door. Sometimes I took advantage of the open door to get out for some exercise. Other times, depending on my mood, I stayed inside. It was safe there.

I had gone through a molt—lost the old snipped off feathers and had nice new ones. I could fly again. Freedom was granted me more often and I took longer and longer flights. I remembered the fun I had at school.

When the big yellow bus came by for the children I was tempted to follow it to school again.

A fellow can resist temptation only so often. Finally I gave in and went back to school. It was just like old times. Screeching children, fun and games, scraps of lunch and all.

I am ashamed to admit it, but I let myself be caught again. Sad to say, I received another coat of paint, too, but not quite such a heavy sticky mess as it was before.

For the second time I was the subject of a school bulletin. This one was written in more severe language.

> "Some very thoughtless, cruel individual or individuals have been spray-painting the tame crow of Forks. The laws of common decency as well as the laws of the state are against this kind of thing. Students knowing who this individual is should make a report to the Humane Society or law enforcement officers."

Though I was very miserable with that awful paint, I hope that the children were made to realize the desirability of being kind to birds and animals

IX. I AM CRIPPLED FOR LIFE

School was out. There had been no children about the grounds for several days. I guess it was Spring Vacation time. It was lonesome for me. I flew about the buildings and would sometimes alight on a windowsill but it was always the same. Just a big empty room with row of desks and clean, blank blackboards on the wall. No children—no noise. I did try to talk to the custodian as he went about from building to building, but he was too busy to pay much attention to me.

Yes, it was quite dull. Of course I did find children about town, in ones and twos. It seemed like they were always going somewhere—and didn't have any lunches either.

I visited various houses where I had been in the habit of getting a bite to eat, and even visited at the bank which was near the school. The big people that worked there were usually willing to toss me a crumb or two—and they didn't try to catch me either.

One afternoon I heard the delightful noise of children at play near the school. Of course I had to investigate. There were two boys in a back yard. They were quite young, perhaps even too young to attend school and not very familiar with me.

I landed in the yard close by these boys and they noticed me right away. Tried to catch me but I was too quick for them. We played together for quite a while. I was really enjoying myself.

I remember picking up a little piece of shiny tin foil and poking about the yard to find a good place to cache it. I suppose my guard was relaxed too much. I didn't watch the children closely—and it was to my eternal sorrow.

Suddenly there was a blinding pain! I felt myself being knocked along the ground and know that I tried to cry out, then all went black. I had fainted.

Gradually I became aware of a throbbing hurt—all over. My head was bent under my wing and my beak was full of dirt and grass. I tried to move. I just couldn't for I was filled with a terrible weakness. I could only lie there with wave after wave of nausea washing over me. I heard a woman's voice scolding:

"You naughty boys! Why did you have to hurt that poor crow! You go home right now!"

Minutes later I was able to twist myself around and get onto my feet. Perhaps I should not say "feet", for one of them did not seem to work. I put it under me but when I attempted to stand I only fell over on my side.

For some reason I was not able to fly either. I beat my wings, but somehow they just were not strong or coordinated enough to lift me from the ground and I flopped over the grass in a most awkward manner.

I do not know how long I trembled there in that back yard. After a while I heard the familiar voices of Dad and Mama and turned to see them approaching. I was sure they meant only good to me but my recent experience had instilled such a fright in me that I tried to avoid them. This awful weakness prevented my escape, however, and soon I found myself in the familiar confines of a cardboard box and on my way back to the Place.

The rest of the day was one of just pure misery. My inoperative leg was broken completely off. (I heard someone say that one of the little boys had hit me with a rake.) My poor leg kept dangling under my body—held only by a shred of skin.

Dad was forced to cut it completely off with a pair of scissors.

I was placed in my own big cage with a pan of water and some of my favorite food. But I could not eat. I was sick and could only squat in a corner of the cage trying to balance on one leg and a stump.

X. I ADJUST TO MY DISABILITY

After many days of rest, good food, and sympathetic treatment, I began to feel like my old self again.

The missing leg is a constant irritation. The skin has pulled back from the severed bone and healed quite well, but I have nothing to grip with on that side—just a stub of bone to clump around on.

Since being freed from the cage I manage quite will at walking around on the ground. A step and a clump, a step and a clump—like that.

My wings have regained their strength and I can sail about the air as well as ever. Making a landing presents a problem. Roofs, large limbs and large fence posts with flat tops I can land quite will on, but small limbs and wires are beyond my ability. I can catch hold with my good foot, but the stub will not hold to small surfaces and I usually find myself floundering and flapping most ungracefully to stay upright.

I find that I must be more cautious in regard to some of my enemies—like strange dogs and cats. With only one foot I am not able to make my former powerful leaps to flight in a hurry, so I must do my teasing and scolding from high flat places (such as fence posts, or from the porch railing.)

As I heard Dad say one day—he was quoting, I am sure:

"Eternal vigilance is the price of liberty."

With relatively small creatures, such as myself, "eternal vigilance" is not only the "price of liberty", it may be the price of life itself.

On Christmas day I sat on one of David's wagons in the back yard of the Place. I don't know why I allowed myself to become so careless, but, anyway, suddenly there was a swish overhead. I leaped for my life and just barely made it to the back porch.

It was old Red-Tail, the hawk. I don't think he missed me by more than the length of one of my primary feathers—but he did.

Yes, I'll just have to be more careful!

Epilogue: We enjoyed our crow so very much! He truly grew to be a part of our family, and has become a treasured and humorous part of our family's history. We never knew what happened in the end to him. He just didn't come home one day and we presume a hawk finally caught him. That is truly sad, but if we hadn't found him as a fledgling, predators would have surely killed him soon after having fallen from his nest. We hope that his story will encourage young people especially to respect and care for nature and the creatures God has put here for us to enjoy.

TEACH Services, Inc.
P U B L I S H I N G

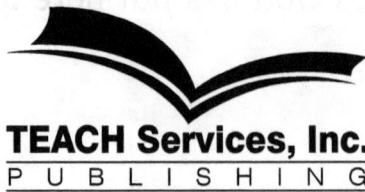

We invite you to view the complete
selection of titles we publish at:
www.TEACHServices.com

We encourage you to write us
with your thoughts about this,
or any other book we publish at:
info@TEACHServices.com

TEACH Services' titles may be purchased in
bulk quantities for educational, fund-raising,
business, or promotional use.
bulksales@TEACHServices.com

Finally, if you are interested in seeing
your own book in print, please contact us at:
publishing@TEACHServices.com

We are happy to review your manuscript at no charge.

www.ingramcontent.com/pod-product-compliance
Lightning Source LLC
Chambersburg PA
CBHW060809110426
42739CB00032BA/3155